"Patience with family is love, patience with others is respect,
patience with self is confidence, patience with God is faith."

— Unknown

"The time of ascension has come for you. Bask in the brilliance of the sun's rays and feel your life ignite. Rejoice in the celebration of you!"

– Ra, Sun God

Rise again, child of light, as the dawn of the new day is with you.

Become the quester of your life. Seek within, and you will discover perceptions, visions, and ways of being you may not have explored thus far.

Where do I seek to grow, yet have not taken the steps to do so?

I am safe to explore the Universe within.

I always have all that I need.

I gift myself with a daily ritual of self-nourishment and care.

I am the great provider in my life.

The language of love is not heard by the ears,
but quite simply felt by the heart.

"You have been created in order that you might make a difference.
You have within you the power to change the world."
–Andy Andrews

"I knew the power of a single wish, after all. Invisible and inevitable, like a butterfly that beats its wings in one corner of the globe and with that single action changes the weather halfway across the world."

— Alice Hoffman

To truly let go, love something wholly and set it free.

Every twenty-eight days, Grandmother Moon shines her full grandness
upon the shadows we have allowed to creep into our hearts.

The spirit of the Bear brings courage and strength to those in need.

The great spirit of the Bear is with me. I draw upon the
strength and courage that lives within me.

At any moment, I can access the calm, the quiet,
and the sweetness that lies within me.

Even amidst what can feel like a constant overflow of
intensity and overstimulation, there is a place of rest and
rejuvenation within. This is your place.

There is a difference between running on adrenalin and
running on energy. For now, be still, replenish your reserves,
and all will be revealed in divine timing.

There is no need to seek love, as it already lives within you.

It is important to fill your own cup regularly before you fill the cup of others.

By loving yourself first, you give the most beautiful gift within this Universe:
The permission for others to love and accept themselves, too.

Self-love is my greatest responsibility.

I recognise my divinity, and I live it.

"Inner tuition" – Within this new world, your pure,
instinctual self is the wayshower of light.

Your inner lotus flower is now open to receiving divine guidance –
follow your intuition.

My voice is a sacred portal to my truth.

When speaking from your heart, there is always love within your words.

Speaking one's truth is a powerful act, and one's actions
reverberate across all levels of space and time.

Allow the gateway of your heart to speak directly through the throat chakra.

"Is it kind, is it true, is it necessary, does it improve upon the silence?"

– Shirdi Sai Baba

Breathe in the limitless love of the universal heart,
and in every breath, know you are perfection.

From this present moment, I see myself as whole and perfect.

Once you choose to live each moment via the love that you are,
the miracle of healing begins to transform every cell in your body
back to the light that it is.

My power is not a force outside of me. My power lives inside of me.

The key to life is to have an absolute, unwavering faith in yourself.

My ideas, my creativity, and my passion matter!

Believe in all you have asked of yourself in this lifetime.
Remember the bigger picture that you chose to play a part in.

In the depths of the night sky, you were born via a divine
spark from the distant constellation you call home.

· The tall ones are guiding you to remember that a tree without
deep roots will not flourish. The same is true for you.